TIMELESS

GREEK

QUOTES

Book n° 4 of the series "Quotes from the World - *A Little Ray of Sunshine* ".

François MARAIN

Dedication

Over to you, dear reader,

This book is dedicated to you. Every page, every word, is designed with the intention of sending a little ray of sunshine into your life. Thank you for allowing these quotes to be a part of your journey.

I am also deeply grateful for the love of my chocolate labrador, who dutifully watches over me as I write. Just looking into those deep, loving eyes keeps me going all day long. It is the visual representation of beauty and love of life.

Kind regards
Francis

Introduction

I really love quotes and sayings from anyone, anywhere – famous people, ordinary people, or the kind of wisdom you hear growing up. They are like little nuggets of intelligence or positivity that can really make you think or cheer you up.

They remind us that we all share this big rock floating in space, called planet Earth. If we could just stop our petty ambitions and greed, we could get along and make life on Earth amazing.

Many thanks to everyone who checked these quotes with me. Your interest counts a lot. I hope these words uplift you and make you smile.

Socrates

Socrates was a classical Greek philosopher who lived around 470-399 BCE and is considered one of the founders of Western philosophy. Unlike many of his contemporaries, Socrates did not write any of his teachings. Instead, what we know about him comes from the writings of his students, such as Plato and Xenophon, as well as the playwright Aristophanes.

Socrates is famous for his contribution to the development of critical thinking and the Socratic method, a technique that involves asking a series of questions to challenge ideas and stimulate deeper understanding. He is known for examining ethical concepts and looking for the underlying essence of virtues like justice and courage.

His philosophy often put him at odds with the Athenian public and its rulers, leading to him being tried and executed for corruption of youth and impiety, or for not believing in the gods of the state. Socrates' insistence on questioning authority and his emphasis on ethics and the importance of the good life had a profound impact on future generations of philosophers, including Plato, who would go on to become Aristotle's mentor, influencing centuries of Western thought.

Despite his execution, Socrates left behind a rich intellectual legacy and is often honored as one of the greatest thinkers in human history. His work continues to be studied and revered for its emphasis on dialogue, ethical living, and the relentless pursuit of knowledge.

Quotes from Socrates

The only true wisdom is to know that you know nothing,

Life that is not examined is not worth living.

There is only one good knowledge and one bad ignorance.

I cannot teach anyone anything, I can only make them think.

To be kind to everyone you meet is to fight a tough battle.

To find yourself, think for yourself.

Strong minds discuss ideas, average minds discuss events, weak minds discuss people.

Education is the lighting of a flame, not the filling of a vase.

Know thyself.

I am neither an Athenian nor a Greek, but a citizen of the world.

The secret to the happiness you see is not in the pursuit of more, but in the development of the ability to enjoy less.

He who is not satisfied with what he has is not satisfied with what he would like to have.

Wisdom begins with wonder.

Do not do to others what makes you angry if you are done by others.

There is only one thing I know, and that is that I do not know anything.

Beware of the sterility of a busy life.

Those who are the hardest to love need it the most.

Understanding a question is a half-answer.

Death is perhaps the greatest of all human blessings.

A man's worth is measured by the number of those who stand by his side, not by those who follow him.

By all means, marry if you have a good wife, you will become happy, if you have a bad one, you will become a philosopher.

Wonder is the beginning of wisdom.

Prefer knowledge to wealth, for the one is transitory, the other perpetual.

Whoever wants to move the world must first move himself.

True knowledge exists in the knowledge that you know nothing.

Despite his execution, Socrates left behind a rich intellectual legacy and is often honored as one of the greatest thinkers in human history. His work continues to be studied and revered for its emphasis on dialogue, ethical living, and the relentless pursuit of knowledge.

Plato

Plato was an ancient Greek philosopher who lived from 427 to 347 BCE and is one of the most influential figures in the development of Western philosophy. He was a pupil of Socrates and later became Aristotle's teacher, forming a fundamental triad of Western philosophical thought.

Plato founded the Academy of Athens, one of the earliest known organized schools in Western civilization, and his work laid the foundation for Western philosophy and science. His writings are in the form of dialogues, with Socrates often serving as a central character who engages others in philosophical discussions. Through these dialogues, Plato explored a wide range of topics, including ethics, politics, metaphysics, and epistemology.

One of Plato's most famous contributions is the theory of forms (or ideas), which posits that the material world as perceived by our senses is not the real world but a shadow of the real world. According to this theory, the real world is composed of immutable and perfect forms that exist in a realm beyond physical reality. Our world is but a reflection of these forms, and true knowledge comes from understanding them.

Plato's best-known work is "The Republic," in which he lays out his vision of an ideal state ruled by philosopher-kings guided by wisdom and justice. This work also contains his famous Allegory of the Cave, a metaphor for the process of enlightenment and the role of the philosopher in society.

Wisdom is the truest form of wealth.

In contact with love, everyone becomes a poet.

A man's measure is what he does with power.

We can easily forgive a child who is afraid of the dark, the real tragedy of life is when men are afraid of the light.

Courage is knowing what not to fear.

One of the penalties for refusing to participate in politics is that you end up being ruled by your inferiors.

Knowledge that is acquired under duress has no hold on the mind.

Necessity is the mother of invention.

The beginning is the most important part of the work.

Ignorance is the root and stem of all evil.

He who commits an injustice is always made more miserable than he who suffers it.

The first and greatest victory is to conquer oneself.

To be afraid of death is just another way of thinking that you are wise when you are not, is to think that you know what you do not know.

No one knows whether death is not the greatest of all blessings to a man, but men fear it as if they knew it to be the greatest of evils.

Good people do not need laws to tell them to act responsibly, while bad people will find a way around the laws.

Music is a moral law. It gives soul to the universe, wings to the mind, flight to the imagination, and charm and gaiety to life and everything.

The heaviest punishment for refusing to govern is to be ruled by someone inferior to oneself.

Thinking about the soul's discourse with itself

Love is a serious mental illness.

Human behavior stems from three main sources: desire, emotion, and knowledge.

Excellence is not a gift but a skill that requires practice. We do not act right because we are excellent; in fact, we achieve excellence by doing the right thing.

The price that good men pay for their indifference to public affairs is to be governed by bad men.

Anything that deceives can be considered an enchantment.

Time is the image of eternity.

Opinion is the medium between knowledge and ignorance.

The soul of man is immortal and imperishable.

Justice is about minding one's own affairs and not meddling in the concerns of others.

Life should be lived as a game.

There are three classes of men: the friends of wisdom, the lovers of honor, and the friends of gain.

Plato's impact on philosophy and the broader scope of Western thought cannot be overstated. His ideas about the nature of knowledge, reality, and the good life have influenced countless philosophers, theologians, and thinkers over the millennia.

Aristotle

Aristotle (384-322 BC) was an ancient Greek philosopher and scientist, one of the most important figures in the intellectual history of the West. He was born in Stagira, in Halkidiki, near Macedonia, and at the age of seventeen he joined Plato's Academy in Athens, where he remained until Plato's death. Aristotle is often portrayed as Plato's most prominent pupil, although he diverged significantly from his master.

After leaving Athens, Aristotle spent some time in Asia Minor, and then served as tutor to Alexander the Great. In 335 B.C., he returned to Athens and founded his own school, the Lyceum, where he spent most of the rest of his life studying, teaching, and writing. His works cover a wide range of subjects, including logic, metaphysics, ethics, politics, rhetoric, poetry, biology, and zoology, reflecting the breadth of his interests and the diversity of his contributions to philosophy and science.

Aristotle's approach to investigation was empirical and systematic, in contrast to Plato's idealist approach. He believed that knowledge comes from experience and that theory should be based on empirical observation and analysis. This methodological approach greatly influenced the development of science, especially during the Renaissance.

Some of Aristotle's most influential ideas include the concept of the golden mean, the idea that virtue lies between two extremes; the theory of the four causes, which are the material, formal, efficient, and final causes; and the categorization of different forms of government. He also made important contributions to ethics, proposing that the purpose of human life should be to attain eudaimonia, often translated as "happiness" or "fulfillment," through the practice of virtuous actions.

Knowing oneself is the beginning of all wisdom.

It is the mark of an educated mind to be able to entertain a thought without accepting it.

What is a friend One soul dwelling in two bodies?

The whole is more than the sum of its parts.

Happiness depends on us.

Whoever has overcome his fears will be truly free.

The roots of education are bitter, but the fruit is sweet.

We are what we do repeatedly, so excellence is not an act but a habit.

The high-minded man must care more about the truth than about what people think.

Patience is bitter but its fruit is sweet.

Pleasure in work puts perfection in work.

It is in our darkest moments that we need to focus on seeing the light.

To avoid criticism, say nothing, do nothing, be nothing.

Man is by nature a political animal.

The purpose of art is not to represent the outward appearance of things, but their inner meaning.

Happiness is the meaning and purpose of life, the goal and end of human existence.

Anyone can get angry, it is easy, but being angry at the right person to the right degree, at the right time, for the right purpose, and in the right way is not easy.

Courage is the first of human qualities because it is the quality that guarantees others.

Poverty is the mother of revolution and crime.

Education is an ornament of prosperity and a refuge from adversity.

To write well, express yourself like ordinary people, but think like a wise man.

It is not enough to win a war; it is more important to organize peace.

Friendship is one soul dwelling in two bodies.

In all things in nature, there is something wonderful.

The educated differ from the uneducated as much as the living differ from the dead.

No great mind has ever existed without a hint of madness.

Hope is a waking dream.

The soul never thinks without an image.

The secret of humor is surprise.

Wishing to be friends is a quick job, but friendship is a fruit that ripens slowly.

Aristotle's impact on Western thought is immense. His works remained influential throughout the Middle Ages and the Renaissance, and he is often referred to as the "father of logic" and the "father of biology." To this day, his work continues to be a crucial reference point for philosophical research and debate.

Homer

Homer is the legendary ancient Greek poet traditionally considered the author of the two oldest and most influential works of Western literature: the Iliad and the Odyssey. These epic poems are at the heart of the ancient Greek canon and have had a huge influence on the history of literature.

The Iliad tells the story of the Trojan War, focusing on a few weeks of the final year of the conflict, and highlights the anger of the warrior Achilles. The Odyssey follows the journey of the hero Odysseus as he attempts to return home to Ithaca after the fall of Troy, a journey that takes him ten years and is filled with fantastic adventures and challenges.

The exact period in which Homer lived is uncertain, with estimates ranging from the twelfth to the eighth centuries BCE. The traditional view is that Homer was a blind bard from Ionia, a region on the west coast of Asia Minor (now Turkey). However, as poems were passed down orally for generations before they were written, there is much scholarly debate about their authorship and the existence of Homer himself. Some suggest that Homer may represent a collective authorial tradition or a synthesis of the tales of a long line of bards.

There is a time for many words and there is also a time for sleep.

Wise to solve and patient to execute.

A man who has had bitter experiences and has traveled far and wide even enjoys his sufferings after a while.

Travel is the thing.

As hateful to me as the gates of Hades is that man who hides one thing in his heart and says another.

Even his sorrows are a joy long after for one who remembers all that he has done and endured.

For a friend with an understanding heart is worth no less than a brother,

It is not unseemly for a man to die fighting in defense of his country.

No one is voluntarily deprived of property.

Few sons are like their fathers, most are worse, little better.

In youth and beauty, wisdom is rare.

There is strength in union, even of very sad men.

A guest never forgets the host who treated them with kindness.

Death is the same in an ordinary person as it is in a king.

Through mutual trust and mutual help, great deeds are accomplished, and great discoveries are made.

The gods envy us They envy us because we are mortal, because any moment can be our last

Light is precious in such a dark world.

Men grow weary of sleep, love, song, and dance sooner than of war.

Let us learn to show our friendship for a man when he is alive and not after his death.

It is easy to descend into Hell night and day, the gates of dark Death are wide open, but to go back, to retrace your steps to the higher air, which is where the problem lies.

All men need the gods.

Often, hatred hurts itself.

The blade itself incites acts of violence.

A woman's advice first led us to misfortune.

Once the damage has been done, even a fool understands it.

I hate this man who hides one thing in his heart and speaks for another.

The imperishable fame will be mine

In the same way, is the generation of leaves the generation of humanity?

It is better to flee from death than to feel its grip.

Despite these uncertainties, Homer's epics have had a lasting impact on Western culture. They are foundational texts in the study of ancient Greek history, mythology, and literature, providing insight into the values, social norms, and ideas of the ancient Greeks. Homer's influence extends beyond literature into art, philosophy, and even the way wars are conceptualized, making him a central figure in the Western literary tradition.

Herodotus

Herodotus, often referred to as the "father of history," was an ancient Greek historian who lived in the fifth century BCE, between 484 and 425 BCE. He was born in Halicarnassus, a Greek city located in what is now Bodrum, Turkey. Herodotus is best known for his work "The Histories", a detailed account of his investigation (or "historía" in Greek, meaning inquiry or inquiry) into the origins and events of the Greco-Persian Wars, as well as his descriptions of the customs, geography, and peoples he encountered during his travels through the Persian Empire, Egypt and other parts of the known world at the time.

"The Stories" is considered the first major work in the history of Western literature. Herodotus set a precedent by systematically gathering his materials, critically evaluating their accuracy to some extent, and then organizing them into a coherent narrative. His work is remarkable not only for its breadth, but also for its in-depth exploration of the cultures and places it describes, offering a glimpse into the ancient world that is invaluable to historians today.

However, Herodotus has also been called the "father of lies" by some critics, ancient and modern, because of the sometimes-fanciful stories included in his Histories. Although he often cited his sources and differentiated between what he believed to be true and what was reported to him, the accuracy of some of his accounts has been questioned.

Quotes from Herodotus

Great actions are usually accomplished at great risk.

Man's destiny is in his own soul.

In peace, sons bury their fathers in war, fathers bury their sons.

Men trust their ears less than they trust their eyes.

Of all the miseries of men, the bitterest is that of knowing so much and controlling nothing.

History is the witness that bears witness to the passing of time, it sheds light on reality, enlivens memory, guides us through daily life and brings us news from antiquity.

Circumstances govern men, men do not govern circumstances.

He is the best man who, when he makes his plans, fears, and thinks about everything that may happen to him, but in the moment of action he is bold.

Very little happens at the right time and the rest doesn't happen at all. Conscientious historians will correct these defects.

It is better, by noble audacity, to run the risk of being subject to half the evils we foresee, than to remain cowardly apathetic for fear of what might happen.

All the gains of men are the fruit of adventure.

Death is a delightful hiding place for weary men.

Strength has no place where skill is needed.

The man who experienced the shipwreck shudders even on a calm sea

Customs are king of all.

Human happiness never stays in one place for long.

It is clear that equality and freedom of expression are a good thing not in one thing, but in many ways.

If a man insists on being stupid, if he does not want to stop, then he should go ahead and be stupid openly.

The most detestable sorrow of all human sorrows is that of having the knowledge of the truth, but no power over the event.

Disease strikes men when they are exposed to change.

Adversity has the effect of giving birth to talents that, under prosperous circumstances, would have remained dormant.

Gods and men are concerned with the end of a war, not its beginning.

Soft Lands Breed Soft Men

Those who are guided by reason generally succeed in their plans, those who are reckless and precipitate seldom enjoy the favor of the gods.

The worst pain a man can suffer is to have a penetrating view of many things and to be able to control nothing.

It is the custom of the Persians to honor those who are nearest to them with the greatest esteem; the farther away they are from them, the less esteemed they are; That is why they hold the king in high esteem, since he is the furthest from them.

Rushing into any business leads to failures.

Despite these criticisms, Herodotus' contribution to the study of history is undeniable. He introduced a narrative form that combined historical facts with cultural anthropology, geography, and ethnography. This comprehensive approach to writing history has influenced countless generations of historians and writers and continues to be a cornerstone in the study of the ancient world.

Thucydides

Thucydides was an ancient Greek historian and a contemporary of Herodotus, but his approach to history and orientation were markedly different. Born around 460 BC, Thucydides is best known for his work "The History of the Peloponnesian War", which chronicles the conflict between Athens and Sparta that took place from 431 to 404 BC. Unlike Herodotus, who included cultural, ethnographic, and mythological explanations in his histories, Thucydides took a more analytical and empirical approach, emphasizing the importance of accuracy and eyewitness testimony.

Thucydides is often considered the father of "scientific history" or "political realism" because he sought to understand the causes of events without resorting to divine intervention, focusing instead on human actions and decisions. He believed that history was cyclical, and that by studying past events, people could more clearly understand present and future events, especially the nature of power, the causes of conflict, and the behaviors of states.

His work is distinguished not only by its rigorous examination of the evidence and analytical approach, but also by its sophisticated narrative structure and the depth of its political and moral ideas. Thucydides delved into the psychology of political leaders, the dynamics of democracy and oligarchy, and the moral complexities of war and power.

"The History of the Peloponnesian War" remains a seminal work in the study of history, political science, and international relations. Thucydides' insistence on accuracy, his skeptical approach to sources, and his analytical framework for understanding human affairs made him an enduring figure in the field of historical scholarship.

The strong do what they can and the weak suffer what they must.

History is the teaching of philosophy by example.

The secret of happiness is freedom, and the secret of freedom is courage.

Ignorance is audacious and knowledge reserved.

Most people, whether in private or public affairs, are more interested in the means than the end.

Power is wielded by those who can instill fear.

The bravest are certainly those who have the clearest vision of what is before them, of glory and danger, and yet go out to meet it.

Justice will exist only where those who are untouched by injustice are filled with the same indignation as those who have been offended.

It is often a misfortune to have very brilliant men at the head of affairs: they expect too much from ordinary men.

We secure our friends not by accepting favors, but by doing them.

Few things are brought to a successful conclusion by an impetuous desire, but most by a calm and prudent foresight.

Freedom is the assured possession of those who have the courage to defend it.

The society that separates its scholars from its warriors will see its thinking made by cowards and its fights by fools.

War is not so much about weapons as it is about money.

Hope is a commodity. It makes more sense to be prepared.

Of all the manifestations of the constraint of power, it is the one that most impresses men.

Self-control is the main element of self-respect and self-respect is the main element of courage.

Men are naturally inclined to acts of charity more than to any other virtue.

A woman's greatest glory is to be less discussed by men, whether they praise or criticize you.

There is no way to avoid war, it can only be postponed to the advantage of others.

Wisdom alone is a science of the other sciences and of itself.

The secret to success is knowing something that no one else knows.

Good fortune is combined with common sense; Bad luck is the result of bad sense.

Be convinced that to be happy is to be free, and that to be free is to be brave.

Revenge is sweeter than life itself, so think fools.

They were born into a world where they were supposed to be soldiers.

The state that separates its scholars from its warriors will see its thinking done by cowards and its fights by fools.

Despite the incompleteness of his work – he stops abruptly in the middle of the narrative – his impact on the methodology and practice of history is profound and lasting.

Euripides

Euripides is one of the three great tragedians of classical Athens, along with Aeschylus and Sophocles. Born around 480 BC, Euripides is said to have written between 92 and 95 plays, 18 of which have survived in their complete form. His work represents the final stage in the evolution of the Athenian tragedy during the fifth century BCE.

Euripides' plays are known for their complex characters, psychological depth, and exploration of inner conflicts, making him a more modern playwright in the eyes of many theatre scholars and practitioners. Unlike his contemporaries, who focused on heroic narratives and the involvement of the gods in human affairs, Euripides often portrayed his characters as ordinary people facing extraordinary circumstances. This emphasis on human emotions and rationality, as well as his use of deus ex machina endings, was innovative at the time and sometimes controversial.

His works explore themes such as the madness of war, the whims of the gods, and the trials of everyday life, often through the lens of mythological narratives. Euripides also gave voice to women and other marginalized members of society, portraying them as complex characters with their own desires, fears, and moral dilemmas. Some of his most famous plays include "Medea," "The Bacchae," "Hippolytus," "Electra," and "The Trojan Women."

"The Trojan Women," for example, is a powerful commentary on the impact of war on women and children, highlighting Euripides' ability to elicit empathy and highlight the human cost of conflict. "Medea," on the other hand, delves deep into themes of revenge, passion, and the position of strangers and women in society, through the story of a woman who takes drastic action against her cheating husband.

Euripides Quotes

Friends show their love in difficult times, not in happiness.

The greatest pleasure in life is love.

Do not waste new tears on old sorrows.

For an aging father, nothing is more expensive than a daughter.

Those whom the gods want to destroy, they first drive mad.

Question everything Learn something Don't answer anything.

The experience of travel is an education in itself.

The wisest men follow their own direction.

Talk common sense to a fool and he calls you a fool.

Happiness is the highest good.

Life has no blessing like a prudent friend.

No one can say for sure that he will still be alive tomorrow.

He who neglects to learn in his youth loses the past and is dead for the future.

Fortune really helps those who have good judgment.

Do not plan business until you have finished what is at hand.

Death is a debt that we all have to pay.

Anger that crosses boundaries causes fear, and excessive kindness eliminates respect.

Silence is the best response to true wisdom.

The company of just and just men is better than wealth and a rich estate.

Where there is no wine, there is no love.

It is not beauty but beautiful qualities that my daughter keeps a husband.

Do not neglect what is nearby aiming for what is far.

Money is the religion of the wise.

Who knows but life is what men call death?

A faithful friend is worth ten thousand relatives.

Intelligence is not wisdom.

Events will take their course: it is useless to be angry with them: he is the happiest who wisely turns them into the best.

Euripides' innovative approach to storytelling and character development had a lasting impact on the development of theatre, influencing not only later Greek playwrights, but also the course of Western literature and theatre. His works continue to be studied and performed today, a testament to their enduring appeal and relevance.

Sophocles

Sophocles (c. 496-406 BCE) is one of the three great tragedians of ancient Greece, along with Aeschylus and Euripides. He is famous for his contributions to Greek tragedy, having written more than 120 plays during his lifetime, although only seven have survived to the present day in their complete form. These surviving works, including "Oedipus Rex," "Antigone," and "Electra," are considered masterpieces of Western literature and remain fundamental to the study of classical Greek drama, literature, and mythology.

Sophocles was born in Colonus, near Athens, and lived through a period of significant political and cultural change in Athens, including its Golden Age and the Peloponnesian War. He was not only a playwright, but also held several important public positions, which testifies to his active participation in the civic life of Athens.

His innovations in the theatre had a significant impact on the development of Greek drama. He increased the number of actors from two to three, which allowed for greater complexity in storytelling and character interaction. This change reduced the role of the chorus in the narrative, focusing more on character development and plot. Sophocles also introduced painted sets and made changes to theatrical production that influenced the dramatic presentation of his plays.

Sophocles' tragedies are known for their exploration of complex moral and philosophical issues, the tragic nature of human existence, and the exploration of fate in relation to free will. "Oedipus Rex," for example, explores themes of fate, guilt, and self-discovery, telling the story of

Oedipus, who unwittingly fulfills a prophecy that he will kill his father and marry his mother. "Antigone" explores themes of law, justice, and individual conscience through the story of Antigone, who defies the king's edict to bury her brother, who is considered a traitor.

Quotes from Sophocles

The strong do what they can and the weak suffer what they must.

History is the teaching of philosophy by example.

The secret of happiness is freedom, and the secret of freedom is courage.

Ignorance is audacious and knowledge reserved.

Most people, whether in private or public affairs, are more interested in the means than the end.

Power is wielded by those who can instill fear.

The bravest are certainly those who have the clearest vision of what is before them, of glory and danger, and yet go out to meet it.

Justice will exist only where those who are untouched by injustice are filled with the same indignation as those who have been offended.

It is often a misfortune to have very brilliant men at the head of affairs: they expect too much from ordinary men.

We secure our friends not by accepting favors, but by doing them.

Few things are brought to a successful conclusion by an impetuous desire, but most by a calm and prudent foresight.

Freedom is the assured possession of those who have the courage to defend it.

The society that separates its scholars from its warriors will see its thinking made by cowards and its fights by fools.

War is not so much about weapons as it is about money.

Hope is a commodity. It makes more sense to be prepared.

Of all the manifestations of the constraint of power, it is the one that most impresses men.

Self-control is the main element of self-respect and self-respect is the main element of courage.

Men are naturally inclined to acts of charity more than to any other virtue.

A woman's greatest glory is to be less discussed by men, whether they praise or criticize you.

There is no way to avoid war, it can only be postponed to the advantage of others.

Wisdom alone is a science of the other sciences and of itself.

The secret to success is knowing something that no one else knows.

Good fortune is combined with common sense; Bad luck is the result of bad sense.

Be convinced that to be happy is to be free, and that to be free is to be brave.

Revenge is sweeter than life itself, so think fools.

They were born into a world where they were supposed to be soldiers.

The state that separates its scholars from its warriors will see its thinking done by cowards and its fights by fools.

His works are celebrated for their deep understanding of the human condition, complex characters, and complex exploration of ethical and moral dilemmas. Sophocles' ability to weave complex themes with deep emotional impact has secured him a central figure in the canon of Western literature.

Pythagoras

Pythagoras was an ancient Greek philosopher and mathematician, born on the island of Samos around 570 BCE. He is best known for the Pythagorean theorem, a fundamental principle of geometry that states that in a right triangle, the square of the length of the hypotenuse (the side opposite the right angle) is equal to the sum of the squares of the lengths of the other two sides. Although this theorem is attributed to Pythagoras, evidence suggests that the Babylonians and Indians knew about this concept long before him.

Beyond mathematics, Pythagoras made important contributions to philosophy and religious education. He is often described as the first pure mathematician and is considered a central figure in the development of mathematics as it is known today. However, his influence extended far beyond this area. Pythagoras founded a religious movement known as Pythagoreanism, which combined aspects of philosophy, science, and religious rites. The Pythagoreans adhered to strict rules and believed in immortality and the transmigration of the soul, living a lifestyle that emphasized ethical purity, mutual loyalty, and the pursuit of philosophical and mathematical studies.

The Pythagoreans contributed significantly to Western thought, particularly by emphasizing the importance of numbers and their belief that the universe could be understood through mathematics. They were among the first to suggest that the Earth was spherical and revolved around a central fire (and not the Sun, as was later discovered). They also explored music theory, understanding the mathematical relationships between musical notes that led to the development of musical scale.

Educate the children and there will be no need to punish the men.

Silence is better than words that do not make sense.

Wisdom well learned will never be forgotten.

Choose to be strong in soul rather than strong in body.

Number is the master of forms and ideas and the cause of gods and demons.

Do not say a little in many words, but a lot in a few.

Above all, respect yourself.

Friends are fellow travelers who should help each other persevere on the path to a happier life.

The strength of the mind rests on sobriety, for it is in this way that your reason is not clouded by passion.

As soon as laws are necessary to men, they are no longer fit for liberty.

Reason is immortal, everything else is mortal.

The oldest, shortest words, yes and no, are the ones that require the most thought.

Pure friendship is something that men of inferior intelligence can never taste.

The fool is known by his words, and the wise by his silence.

In anger, we must refrain from both speaking and acting.

Just do the right thing and let others talk about you the way they want.

There is geometry in the hum of the strings, there is music in the spacing of the spheres.

The most beautiful and profound experience is the sensation of the mystic.

It is difficult to walk several paths of life at the same time.

The wind blows over the sea.

Virtue is harmony.

Salt is born from the purest parents, the sun, and the sea.

If there is light, then there is darkness, if there is heat, warmth, height, depth, if it is solid, fluid, if it is hard, soft, so rough, smooth, if it is a calm storm, a storm, a prosperity, an adversity, a life, a death.

Do not even think about doing what should not be done.

Despise all those things which you will not lack when they are released from the body.

Justice consists in not harming the decency of men, in not offending them.

Demosthenes

Demosthenes is best known for his Philippics, a series of speeches that opposed the expansionist policies of Philip II of Macedon, father of Alexander the Great. Through these speeches, he sought to incite the Athenian public and the other Greek city-states to unite and oppose Macedonian rule. His oratorical efforts culminated in the unsuccessful attempt to rally Greece against the conquests of Alexander the Great.

Despite his ultimate failure to stop Macedonia's rise to power, Demosthenes' speeches have been celebrated throughout the ages for their rhetorical brilliance and depth of political acumen. His work has had a lasting impact on the fields of rhetoric and public speaking, influencing not only subsequent generations in antiquity, but also the development of public speaking in Western culture to the present day.

Small opportunities are often the beginning of big ventures.

The man who has received a benefit must always remember it, but the one who has bestowed it must immediately forget it.

Nothing is easier than deceiving yourself. For what every man desires, which he also believes to be true.

Reminding a man of the good tricks you have performed on him is just like a reproach.

The word is a mirror of the soul: as man speaks, so too does man.

Action and care will eventually exhaust the strongest body, but guilt and melancholy are poisons of quick dispatch.

What we would like us to believe willingly

Excessive relations with tyrants are not good for the security of free states.

An easy life brings few examples of virtue.

For those who wish to persuade people, the trust of their listeners is essential.

The beginning accounts for more than half of the whole.

Demosthenes' life ended in tragedy when he was forced to flee Athens to escape Macedonian rule. He eventually committed suicide to avoid capture, ending the life of one of Athens' most passionate and eloquent defenders. His legacy, however, lives on through his speeches, which continue to be studied for their linguistic art and insight into the political challenges of his time.

Archimedes

Archimedes of Syracuse (c. 287 BC – c. 212 BCE) was an ancient Greek mathematician, physicist, engineer, inventor, and astronomer. Widely regarded as one of the greatest scientists of classical antiquity and one of the greatest mathematicians of all time, Archimedes made profound contributions that laid the foundation for much of modern science and mathematics.

Born in the city of Syracuse on the island of Sicily, Archimedes was instrumental in the development of mathematics. He is known for his work in geometry, particularly for calculating the area under a curve, determining the area and volume of spheres, cylinders, and other shapes, and for using the exhaustion method to approximate the value of pi with remarkable accuracy.

In physics, Archimedes is famous for formulating the principle of buoyancy, known as Archimedes' principle. This principle states that a body immersed in a fluid is supported by a force equal to the weight of the fluid displaced by the body, which is a fundamental law of physics and engineering.

Archimedes is also famous for his inventions. He designed innovative machines, including war machines to defend Syracuse from invasion. Among his contributions were the screw pump, known as Archimedes' screw, used to raise water for irrigation and other purposes, and compound pulley systems for lifting heavy objects, which demonstrated the principle of mechanical advantage.

One of the most famous anecdotes about Archimedes is how he discovered the principle of displacement while taking a bath and realized that he could use it to determine whether a crown was made of pure gold or gold-silver alloy without destroying it. Apparently, he was so excited by this discovery that he ran naked through the streets exclaiming "Eureka!" (I found it!).

Archimedes Quotes

Give me a place to stand and I will stir up the earth.

Eureka! I found it.

The shortest distance between two points is a straight line.

Objects immersed in fluid experience a buoyancy force equal to the weight of the fluid being displaced.

Do not disturb my circles.

There are things that seem unbelievable to most men who have not studied mathematics.

Mathematics reveals its secrets only to those who approach it with pure love, for their own beauty.

Those who claim to discover everything, but produce no proof, can be refuted as having really claimed to discover the impossible

The rising waters lift all ships.

Nature abhors a vacuum.

To measure is to know

The weight of the king's crown can be determined by the movement of the water.

Infinite things are innumerable.

The greatest flaw of the human race is our inability to understand exponential function.

Miracles are not contrary to nature, but only contrary to what we know about nature.

Understanding is more important than knowledge.

There is no room for chance in our reasoning.

Archimedes died during the Roman siege of Syracuse, apparently killed by a Roman soldier despite orders not to harm him. His work remained influential for centuries, providing a rich source of ideas for scientists and mathematicians during the Renaissance and beyond. Archimedes' mathematical theories, inventions, and methods left a lasting legacy, exemplifying the power of human thought and ingenuity.

Hippocrates

Hippocrates of Kos (c. 460 BC – c. 370 BCE) was an ancient Greek physician who is often referred to as the "Father of Medicine" in recognition of his lasting contributions to the field as the founder of the Hippocratic School of Medicine. This intellectual school revolutionized medicine in ancient Greece, establishing it as a discipline distinct from other fields with which it had traditionally been associated (such as theurgy and philosophy), thus making medicine a profession.

Unlike many of his contemporaries and predecessors, Hippocrates based his medical practice on the observation and study of the human body. He believed that the disease had a physical and rational explanation and rejected the common view of the time that disease was caused by superstitions, possession by spirits, or punishment by the gods. Hippocrates and his followers were among the first to describe diseases based on symptoms and categorize diseases into acute, chronic, endemic, and epidemic.

One of Hippocrates' most enduring contributions is the Hippocratic Oath, a set of ethical guidelines for physicians that emphasizes principles such as confidentiality and non-maleficence. Although the original oath has been modified over the centuries, its spirit remains a cornerstone of medical ethics today.

Hippocrates also made important contributions to the systematic study of clinical medicine, summarizing the medical knowledge of the earlier schools and prescribing practices for physicians through his Hippocratic Corpus, a collection of about 70 works, although it is debated which of these were written by him personally. These texts cover a wide range of topics, from diagnosis and surgery to gynecology and pharmacology.

His approach to medicine and disease, known as the humoral theory, postulates that health is maintained by a balance of four bodily fluids or "humors": blood, phlegm, black bile, and yellow bile. The disease was thought to result from an imbalance in these humors, and treatment was aimed at restoring balance, often through diet and lifestyle changes.

Hippocratic Quotes

It is more important to know what kind of person has a disease than it is to know what type of disease a person has.

Let food be your medicine and medicine be your food.

Walking is man's best medicine.

There are actually two things, science, and opinion; The former begets knowledge, the latter ignorance.

Extreme remedies are very suitable for extreme diseases.

Prayer is good, it is good, but in invoking the gods, man himself must lend a hand.

Get into the habit of two things: help; or at least not to do any harm.

Anything in excess is opposed to nature.

Healing is a matter of time, but sometimes it is also a matter of opportunity.

The natural forces within us are the true healers of disease.

Doing nothing is sometimes a good remedy.

The natural healing force in each of us is the greatest force for recovery.

A doctor who has no knowledge of astrology has no right to call himself a doctor.

Diseases are crises of purification, of toxic elimination.

Water, air, and cleanliness are the principal articles of my pharmacopoeia.

Hippocrates' emphasis on ethical care and observation had a lasting impact on the practice of medicine, and his name is still invoked in the Hippocratic Oath taken by new physicians. His work represents a pivotal moment in the history of medicine, marking a shift towards practices based on empirical observation and humanism.

Greek Proverbs and Sayings

The camel does not see its hump.

A friend in need is a friend, even an enemy of the wise.

The eyes we do not see are quickly forgotten,

Rush is wasteful.

A fish rots from head down.

Better an hour of freedom than forty years slavery and prison.

The drowned man clings to his hair to get out of his way.

water.

It is for the health of the wolf, so that his mother does not.

Do not cry.

A good captain reveals himself in the storm.

What does not kill you makes you stronger.

Many opinions sink the ship,

Big words do not get through doors.

Where you hear a lot of cherries, take a small basket with you.

The tongue has no bones, but it breaks bones.

One thing in its own time, and radishes at Easter.

When the cat is away, the mice will play.

It is the pot that calls for the black kettle.

It is all fair in love, war, and backgammon.

Life is like riding a bike, to keep your balance, you have to keep moving.

Conclusion

If you liked this book...

Thank you for reading this book!

I really appreciate all the feedback and would really appreciate your input to improve the next version of this book. Please take two minutes now to leave a review on Amazon, it helps tremendously:

2mindspublishing.com/review

Thank you very much!

Francis

Copyright

omissions are the result of negligence. an accident or any other cause. Compliance with all applicable laws and regulations, including international, federal, state, and local professional licenses, business practices, advertising, and all other aspects of conducting business in the United States, Canada, or any other jurisdiction is the sole responsibility of the reader and the consumer.

Neither the author nor the publisher assumes any liability of any kind on behalf of the consumer or reader of such material. Any unintentional offense against an individual or organization is purely unintentional.

The resources in this book are provided for informational purposes only and should not be used as a substitute for the specialized training and professional judgment of a health or mental health professional.

Neither the author nor the publisher can be held responsible for the use of the information provided in this book. Please always consult a qualified professional before making any decisions about your treatment or the treatment of others. For more information, email fm@2mindspublishing.com

Table of Contents